Coaching for High Performance

How to develop exceptional results through coaching

SARAH COOK

Soft Skills for
IT Professionals

IT Governance Publishing

Every possible effort has been made to ensure that the information contained in this book is accurate at the time of going to press, and the publishers and the author cannot accept responsibility for any errors or omissions, however caused. No responsibility for loss or damage occasioned to any person acting, or refraining from action, as a result of the material in this publication can be accepted by the publisher or the author.

Apart from any fair dealing for the purposes of research or private study, or criticism or review, as permitted under the Copyright, Designs and Patents Act 1988, this publication may only be reproduced, stored or transmitted, in any form, or by any means, with the prior permission in writing of the publisher or, in the case of reprographic reproduction, in accordance with the terms of licences issued by the Copyright Licensing Agency. Enquiries concerning reproduction outside those terms should be sent to the publishers at the following address:

IT Governance Publishing
IT Governance Limited
Unit 3, Clive Court
Bartholomew's Walk
Cambridgeshire Business Park
Ely
Cambridgeshire
CB7 4EH
United Kingdom

www.itgovernance.co.uk

First published in the United Kingdom in 2009
by IT Governance Publishing.

ISBN 978-1-84928-002-0

FOREWORD

IT is often seen as a 'hard-skill' profession where there is no place for soft skills. Yet the importance of soft skills for the IT professional should not be underrated; they underlie all behaviours and interactions. Both IT and non-IT professionals need to work together and learn from each other for effective business performance. All professionals, be they in IT or elsewhere, need to understand how their actions and reactions impact on their behaviour and working relationships.

This series of books aims to provide practical guidance on a range of soft-skills areas for those in IT and also for others, including those who deal with IT professionals, in order to facilitate more effective and co-operative working practices.

Each book is written by an experienced consultant and trainer. Their approach throughout is essentially practical and direct, offering a wealth of tried and tested professional guidance. Each chapter contains focused questions to help the coach plan and steer their course. The language used is jargon-free, and a bibliography and a helpful glossary of terms are included at the end of the book.

Angela Wilde, January 2009

PREFACE

This book is intended to provide IT managers with practical advice and tips on how to create a coaching environment in their department.

Coaching is a powerful tool to create high performance in all IT teams. *Fortune* magazine found that, asked for a conservative estimate of the monetary payoff from coaching, managers who had been coached described an average return of more than $100,000, or about six times what the coaching cost them in time, money and effort.

Coaching is a forward-focused activity. It helps people improve their performance and enhance the quality of their work. Plus, it is a skill that is readily usable by all. It is a set of behaviours that you can adopt during a five-minute chat with a colleague, in a direct report, during a one-to-one meeting or a performance review, or as part of an IT project meeting.

In reading this book, I hope that you will be inspired to apply the coaching skills to your IT workplace to help you create an environment of high performance.

Sarah Cook

The Stairway Consultancy Ltd

www.thestairway.co.uk

ABOUT THE AUTHOR

Sarah Cook is the Managing Director of the Stairway Consultancy Ltd. She has 15 years' consulting experience specialising in executive coaching, leadership and change. Prior to this, Sarah worked for Unilever and as Head of Customer Care for a retail marketing consultancy.

As well as having practical experience of coaching individuals in public- and private-sector organisations to enhance their personal effectiveness and optimise their performance, Sarah is a business author and has written widely on the topic of leadership, management development, coaching and team-building. She also speaks regularly at conferences and seminars on these topics.

Sarah is a Fellow of the Chartered Institute of Personnel and Development and a Chartered Marketeer. She has an MA from Cambridge University and an MBA. Sarah is an accredited user of a wide range of psychometric and personal diagnostic tools. She may be contacted via _sarah@thestairway.co.uk_.

ACKNOWLEDGEMENTS

I wish to acknowledge:

Sir John Whitmore, whose GROW model of coaching is widely accepted as best practice. See *Coaching For Performance: Growing People, Performance and Purpose* (3rd revised edition, Nicholas Brealey Publishing Ltd, 2002)

Laura Whitworth, Henry Kimsey-House, Karen Kimsey-House and Phil Sandahl for their 3 Levels of Listening model. See *Co-active Coaching: New Skills for Coaching People Toward Success in Work and Life* (Davies Black, 2007)

Peter Hawkins of the Bath Consulting Group, whose CLEAR is a model for coaching (*www.bath consultancygroup.com*)

Tim Gallwey, the founder of coaching as we know it today. See *The Inner Game of Tennis* (Pan, 1975).

CONTENTS

CHAPTER 1: WHAT IS COACHING?

In this chapter I provide you with:

- A definition of coaching and how this is different to training, counselling and mentoring.
- An overview of the benefits of coaching.
- An illustration of where coaching may be useful for you.
- An overview of how coaching is linked to performance management.

Too much to do, too little time

Marvin was struggling. Although an experienced IT manager, he was new to the organisation. He had inherited a department consisting of a mixture of 'old hands' as well as several graduates and project managers who, like himself, were new to the organisation. The business had an aggressive agenda for change encompassing several major IT projects. The trouble was, although everyone had the best of intentions, no one on Marvin's team seemed to be pulling their weight. Deadlines were being missed, tempers were becoming frayed and Marvin seemed to end up doing more and more of the work himself in order to keep things afloat.

Marvin realised that something had to change if his department was going to achieve the Key Performance Indicators it had been set. In desperation, Marvin called one of his former colleagues who was now heading a successful IT team in another firm. How, he wanted to know, had his ex-colleague been so successful in creating a high-performance team?

And this is how Marvin discovered the benefits of coaching. This book shares Marvin's journey of discovery; it outlines what coaching is, the benefits of coaching, the process and skills of coaching and how it can be used successfully in an IT environment to bring about sustained levels of high performance, personal achievement and growth.

My hope is that in reading this book you will benefit from the power of coaching.

What is coaching?

There are various definitions of coaching:

- 'An ongoing professional relationship that helps people achieve extraordinary results'
- 'Helping people to unlock their potential'
- 'The process of accelerating an individual's progress to achieving personal and organisational goals'
- 'The partnership between a manager and an individual, whereby the manager helps the individual to learn'.

In essence, coaching is forward-looking and goal-oriented. The purpose of coaching is to help individuals define desired outcomes for themselves, to create awareness of the options open to them in achieving their desired outcomes and to help them take responsibility for developing appropriate strategies and actions to achieve them.

1: What Is Coaching?

Coaching versus other disciplines

Coaching is different to training as the latter involves teaching something, usually a skill. The coaching process assumes that the coachee has the ability to find the resources they need to achieve their goal. Coaching is about helping people to learn, rather than teaching them.

Coaching is also different to counselling as it is forward-focused and goal oriented, whereas counselling tends to focus on the past. Counselling typically helps people to work through problems in their past which are impacting their current performance.

Coaching is different to mentoring as mentoring usually involves a more experienced person offering advice and acting as a role model to others. In coaching the coach does not have to know the answers as their role is to help the coachee find their own way.

Coaching	Counselling
Focus on a goal	Focus on a difficulty
Direction is to achieve the goal	Direction is to overcome the difficulty
Future-focused	Focused on the past
Discussion around possibilities	Discussion around problems
Clarifies objectives, encourages action	Focus on healing

Solution-oriented	Fixes the 'problem'
Coach helps the coachee move towards a solution	Counsellor helps the client move away from a problem

Table 1: Key differences between coaching and counselling

What are the benefits of coaching?

Coaching is a proven way of improving performance in a business setting. It is a technique that all IT professionals will find invaluable. One of the benefits of coaching is that it can be applied to many settings and undertaken in as short a time as fifteen minutes.

Fortune magazine undertook a survey in 2006 regarding the benefits to companies that encouraged coaching. Its research found that coaching resulted in increases in:

- productivity (reported by 53% of respondents)
- quality (48%)
- organisational strength (48%)
- customer service (39%).

Respondents also reported benefits in the following areas:

- reducing customer complaints (34%)
- retaining executives who received coaching (32%)
- cost reductions (23%)
- bottom-line profitability (22%).

Where coaching can be of benefit to you

Listed below are a variety of situations that you may face in your role within IT. Consider those that may apply to you:

Applicable?	Yes/No?
Improving working relationships with direct reports	
Improving working relationships with immediate line manager	
Improving working relationships with peers	
Improving working relationships with customers	
Improving working relationships with other stakeholders	
Developing a high-performance team	
Dealing with underperformance	
Developing others	
Managing talent	
Enhancing your career	
Resolving conflict	
Improving personal effectiveness	
Improving confidence	

Raising your profile	
Enhancing job satisfaction	
Improving life–work balance	

Table 2: Coaching situations

The good news is that coaching can help you address all these issues and more.

When, where and whom to coach

Coaching is a tool that can be used at any time and in any place, via telephone, e-mail and face to face. As an IT manager there are a wide number of people that you may be able to coach, ranging from team members and colleagues to key stakeholders. (Using the models and approaches in this book you will also be able to coach yourself!)

My own experience of coaching others has spanned helping individuals with improving their confidence, creating a greater impact at work, managing their careers and succession planning, through to managing interpersonal relationships and helping others improve their performance.

You can coach during the working day, before or after work, at lunch, during a break, at a workstation, off site, on the telephone, face to face or via e-mail. Coaching is a skill that you can also apply out of work with family and friends.

Coaching as part of performance management

Coaching and feedback sit at the heart of the performance management cycle. It should be an ongoing and regular event.

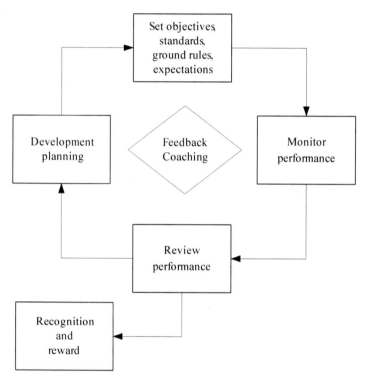

Figure 1: The performance management cycle

The performance management cycle starts with the manager setting clear objectives, ground rules and expectations. He or she monitors and reviews performance as well as encouraging the creation of development plans, providing reward and recognition. Coaching and feedback sit at the heart of performance management as they are interventions that you can use at any stage. For example, as a manager you can coach people around

- managing talent and developing potential,
- creating personal development plans and
- building on people's strengths.

Coaching is also a powerful tool to help you manage poor performance and underperformance.

Organisations such as Sears in the US have used coaching as part of their performance management process on an ongoing basis. In an article in the *Harvard Business Review*, authors Rucci, Kim and Quinn discuss how coaching contributed to the turnaround of Sears: 'In their "turnaround" effort, the company's mission was to have Sears be a "compelling place to work, a compelling place to shop, and compelling place to invest"'.

They set up rigorous measurements for (among other things) employee attitude and satisfaction. One of their primary questions was, 'How does the way you are treated by those who supervise you influence your overall attitude about your job?' Their statistics showed consistently that as the quality of management improved, so did employee attitudes, and then customer satisfaction. The numbers showed that 'a 5 point improvement in employee attitudes will drive a 1.3 point improvement in customer satisfaction, which in turn will drive a 0.5% improvement in revenue growth'.

In a billion-dollar company, 0.5% increase in revenue is substantial. Sears learned that when their managers fully value and develop their employees (i.e. using the coaching approach), they could confidently predict future revenue growth in a particular district. When employee satisfaction increased 5%, revenue growth in a particular store increased by 5.5%.

Summary

Coaching is a forward-focused and goal-oriented tool that can help you improve the performance of individuals on your team. In addition, it can help you resolve issues you may face with colleagues, key stakeholders or even your boss. In adopting a coaching approach, you are more likely to achieve high levels of both employee engagement and customer satisfaction. This book is designed to provide practical techniques on how you can achieve this.

At the end of each chapter is a series of questions that you might want to reflect on personally or use as the basis for department or team discussions. In addition, any of these questions might serve as the basis for IT/stakeholder conversations prior to you introducing coaching.

- How does the definition of coaching this book provides differ from your own?
- What do you and others perceive to be the key benefits of coaching in your IT department?
- Which people in your department could benefit from coaching and in which areas?
- How can you integrate coaching into your company's performance management cycle?
- How could you personally benefit from coaching?

CHAPTER 2: THE SKILLS AND STYLES OF COACHING

In this chapter I discuss:

- What are the skills of coaching?
- How do your current skills measure up?
- The underlying beliefs of the effective coach and the coachee.
- Three styles of coaching and when they are appropriate.

Introduction

Having identified what coaching is and the potential benefits this brings, in this chapter I will focus on the skills and beliefs of the effective coach. I will also discuss the context in which you as IT manager are likely to coach and therefore the style of coaching which is likely to be most beneficial.

The skills of coaching

I was recently working with the IT manager of a large organisation who wanted to introduce coaching to her team. The solution she had come up with was to ask for a proposal from an external coaching organisation to come in to act as coach. Her boss had refused the investment and asked her to think again. On discussion it appeared that the IT manager was under the impression that coaching was an expertise that needed to come from outside the organisation. In fact, during my discussion with her I helped her realise that she had many of the skills needed to become a good coach herself. Indeed, with some training, help and guidance, she and her colleagues delivered a coaching programme that resulted in improving the performance of her and her colleagues' teams.

So, what are the skills of coaching?

Coaching is a process that encourages self-discovery. It generates solutions and strategies that the coachee takes ownership of and responsibility for. The key skills you will need as a coach therefore centre around establishing trust and rapport with the coachee, communicating effectively and facilitating learning and results.

Establishing rapport and trust is a key skill of the coach because this is the foundation of effective coaching. If the person who is being coached does not feel rapport with their coach, they are not likely to trust them, share their confidences or move forward towards their goals.

Trust and rapport help generate a safe and supportive environment that is respectful and open. In order to achieve this, the coach

- is honest and sincere,
- demonstrates genuine concern for the coachee's welfare,
- establishes a strong contract or way of working with the coachee,
- keeps their promises,
- shows respect towards the coachee,
- demonstrates supportive behaviours to offer encouragement and build confidence and

- questions and encourages appropriate risk-taking in the coachee in order to stretch their thinking and encourage personal development.

By building trust and rapport you can encourage the coachee to open up. The coachee may not be used to talking about themselves and be cautious at first about doing so. When the coachee feels that you as the coach demonstrate genuine respect and concern for them, they are more likely to be comfortable in discussing their performance.

Communicating effectively involves active listening, questioning, observation and feedback skills. As a coach you need to listen actively to what the coachee is saying. This means focusing totally on what the coachee is saying in order to understand the context about which the coachee is talking. As we will see in later chapters, listening has a number of levels. To coach effectively you will need to listen to the words that the coachee uses as well as pick up their underlying meanings. The skilled coach picks up what is not being said as well as what is being said by the coachee.

Linked to listening is effective questioning. By questioning you raise the coachee's awareness of the current situation. Additionally effective questioning helps generate responsibility in the coachee for the actions that they are going to take. Powerful questions help move the coachee forward. They create greater clarity, options and new learning.

Observation and feedback skills are important, too. This means that as the coach you need to use direct language, be respectful of the coachee and offer observations and insights to help the individual develop.

Facilitating learning and results centres on helping the coachee identify major strengths and options for development as well as evaluating these options. It is about the ability to help the coachee take responsibility for new actions and behaviours that move them to their coaching goals.

These skills remain the same whether you coach face to face or on the telephone. The only exception is that you cannot see the other person if you are coaching on the telephone! This means your listening skills become more important. Remember to focus on what the person is saying and not to become distracted by other things around you if you are coaching on the phone.

How do your current skills measure up?

Use the following self-assessment tool to identify what your strengths are in terms of the skills of coaching and where your development areas lie.

Below is a list of statements regarding the different skills needed in coaching.

Read each statement and thinking about your behaviour in a group, tick the number which best agrees with your assessment of your skills, where

1　disagree strongly
2　disagree
3　neither agree or disagree
4　agree
5　agree strongly.

1	I find it easy to get on with most people	1	2	3	4	5
2	When I meet people with differing views to mine, I am always understanding of their perspective	1	2	3	4	5
3	When I meet new people I quickly establish a relationship	1	2	3	4	5
4	People know I am listening to them	1	2	3	4	5
5	I find it easy to let people have their say	1	2	3	4	5
6	I am a listener rather than a talker	1	2	3	4	5
7	I make good use of open questions to establish facts	1	2	3	4	5
8	My questions follow the agenda of the other person	1	2	3	4	5
9	I am not afraid to probe for underlying feelings and concerns when I feel it is appropriate	1	2	3	4	5
10	I find it easy to observe detail	1	2	3	4	5
11	I back up my intuition with observations	1	2	3	4	5
12	I can effectively interpret body language	1	2	3	4	5
13	I deliver feedback directly and concisely	1	2	3	4	5

14	I use my observations to deliver evidence-based feedback	1	2	3	4	5
15	I deliver a balance of both motivational and developmental feedback	1	2	3	4	5
16	I encourage others to consider all options before coming to a solution	1	2	3	4	5
17	I provide a sounding board to help others evaluate the options	1	2	3	4	5
18	I ensure that other people take responsibility for their actions	1	2	3	4	5

Table 3: Assess your coaching skills

Now look at your scores. Add the following questions together:

Questions 1, 2 and 3, which relate to developing trust and rapport, score out of 15:   _____

Questions 4, 5 and 6, which relate to listening, score out of 15:   _____

Questions 7, 8 and 9, which relate to questioning, score out of 15:   _____

Questions 10, 11 and 12, which relate to observation, score out of 15:   _____

Questions 13, 14 and 15, which relate to providing feedback, score out of 15:   _____

Questions 16, 17 and 18, which relate to facilitating learning and results, score out of 15:   _____

How to interpret your score

The average score for this questionnaire is 12 for each section. Therefore a score lower than this indicates that you need to increase your competence in this area. Above this score and you should already have the skills to help you become an effective coach – but practice always makes perfect!

Look at the score for each section. Highlight your highest scores. Congratulate yourself on these skills.

Highlight your lowest scores. Use the chapters in this book to help you develop a plan of action to improve these skills.

The underlying beliefs of the effective coach and coachee

In order to coach effectively, we need to be aware of the underlying beliefs and attitudes that are helpful when coaching. If, for example, we believe that the individual we are coaching is not capable of learning or developing themselves, it is unlikely that the coaching will result in a positive output. Our own beliefs will affect the attitude we take to the coaching, and therefore also the approach that we take and the behaviours we display towards the coachee.

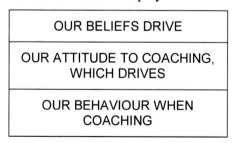

Figure 2: Our beliefs drive our behaviour

Beliefs which are helpful in coaching centre on aspects such as:

- The coachee wants to be coached.
- The coachee has the ability to learn and develop.
- The responsibility for learning and development lies with the coachee.
- Mistakes are a learning opportunity.
- The coach is there to help provide clarity of purpose, not to judge the individual.
- Coaching helps the individual uncover new perspectives and raises their awareness.
- Coaching is coachee-lead – it is not about the coach's agenda but rather about the coachee's.
- Coaching is about facilitating self-directed learning.

Having read this list, it may be useful to challenge yourself around the beliefs you hold about coaching and the assumptions you make about the coaching relationship.

The styles of coaching and when they are appropriate

The assumptions that you make about coaching will probably be visible in the coachee by the style of coaching that you adopt. There are three styles of coaching:

Directing

This is where you, as the coach, like to retain control. You set targets with the coachee, provide solutions and give clear and detailed instructions.

You work closely with the coachee, check their understanding and give feedback on progress.

This style of coaching will work well when the coachee is new to a task or situation or there is only one way of doing a task.

Guiding

Here you, as the coach, retain some control, but allow the learner as much freedom as they feel comfortable with. You typically discuss and explore issues with the coachee. You help the coachee to evaluate options, giving your opinion as one of those options. You tend only to get involved with the coachee at their request.

Guiding will work well in situations where the coachee has the basic knowledge or skill and needs to improve their confidence and competence.

Empowering

The empowering style of coaching is where you, as coach, are involved in helping the coachee to manage their own learning. You typically use open questions to help the coachee think things through for themselves and come up with their own solutions and ways forward. You act as a sounding board for the coachee. The coachee takes responsibility and accountability for their performance.

Empowering will work well when the coachee is competent but not confident in a particular area or when there is not only one answer or way of doing something.

The danger is that often the easiest approach to adopt when coaching is a directing style. As managers this style is often be easiest to adopt, and in the moment it can seem the quickest and most efficient. However, as this is clearly a 'tell' approach to coaching, the downside of which is that the coachee does not take responsibility for their own learning. It becomes easier for them to ask the manager how to do something than to take ownership of finding this out themselves. Using a directing style of coaching implies that you are the expert. The coachee needs to follow the coach's agenda to success. There is no flexibility for the coachee to explore their own options and to discover for themselves.

Summary

In this chapter I have outlined the skills of coaching and provided you with a self-assessment diagnostic of your own skills. I have also outlined the underlying beliefs helpful to being effective coach and the directing, guiding and empowering styles of coaching. In the following chapters you will see that the approach which I advocate to coaching uses a co-operative and empowering style. It is my belief that these two styles bring the biggest rewards in terms of coaching. In the following chapters I set out how you can go about this.

Here are some questions to ask yourself and others in relation to your own and others' skills and style of coaching:

- Which of the skills of coaching do you find most easy to use? Which are the most difficult? How can you develop the skills which you find hardest?

- What beliefs do you personally hold about coaching? How do these limit or enhance your potential coaching relationships? What assumptions do you or others in your organisation make about how people learn best? How do these relate to coaching?
- What are your thoughts on which style of coaching will be most useful in an IT environment?

CHAPTER 3: MODELS OF COACHING

In this chapter I set out:

- The history of coaching and how it has become an established management tool.
- Four different models of coaching and how you can apply them when you are coaching.

The history of coaching

Have you ever wondered how coaching came to be established as a well-known performance technique? Are you confused by the wealth of terminology surrounding coaching, such as executive coaching, life coaching, career coaching, fitness coaching, etc?

Coaching as we know it began in the 1970s when a Harvard graduate called Tim Gallwey was doing some tennis coaching. It was getting late and Gallwey was monotonously throwing balls for students to hit. Lost in reverie, Gallwey noticed that the students appeared to be improving their own game in spite of Gallwey not giving them instructions. He noticed that what appeared to be happening was that students were subconsciously realising their own potential.

He recognised that often, when playing tennis, the coachees experienced 'interference' from their own internal self-talk; the coachees were telling themselves, for example, 'that's a bad shot', 'that won't work', 'remember to lift your racquet'. He called this state 'Self 1'. What he called 'Self 2' is the state of high-performance flow that allows us to be at our best. He identified that 'Self 2' can be accessed by moving the coachee into a state of focused relaxation where the internal dialogue of 'Self 1' is removed. By using open questions to generate awareness, like 'what do you notice?', 'where are you looking?', Gallwey found that individuals realised their own potential.

Gallwey went on to write several books outlining his coaching theory, including *The Inner Game of Tennis* and *The Inner Game of Golf*. His theories of self-directed learning by raising awareness and creating responsibility helped establish the non-directive coaching movement that we see today.

The approach to performance coaching was taken up in the UK by Sir John Whitmore. A former racing driver, he developed a model of self-directed coaching called GROW which is now the approach used by business coaches across the world. We will explore the GROW model later in this chapter. It is based on the principle, developed by Gallwey, of 'teaching people how to learn'. It uses open questions to help the coachee raise their own awareness of the current state and future options.

In the current decade, coaching has been integrated into businesses as a recognised tool for releasing potential. The coaching profession has now come of age. It is now self-regulated and organisations employ external coaches or training them internally.

So which coaching models can you use in an IT environment?

Models of coaching

Coaching is a process that anyone can learn. There are various models of coaching that can help you to coach. These are underpinned by the skills of coaching that we will discuss in further chapters.

Here is an overview of four models of coaching that you may find useful. These are:

- GROW
- STAR
- CIGAR
- CLEAR.

The GROW model

The GROW model of coaching, developed by Sir John Whitmore, uses a series of open questions to help the individual raise their awareness and increase responsibility for and ownership of their actions and behaviours. GROW is a mnemonic that stands for

- Goal
- Reality
- Options
- Will or Way Forward.

The key to using this sequence effectively is to be flexible as a coach; for example, you may reach the second or third stage, then find the need to backtrack and redefine the goal. The flexible coach will use the guide in a dynamic way to match the needs of the coachee.

You will also notice that an important stage in the process is Reality: where the coachee is now. Whitmore, like Gallwey before him, found that typically in conversations people talk about the past, discuss their goal going forward and then move straight to the future. Gallwey found that by encouraging the coachee to focus on what is happening now, he made it possible for people to look at their performance from a different perspective. This brought them insights and harnessed their intuition, which allowed them to generate options and actions for the future.

Here is a description of the key stages of the GROW process:

Goal

- Ask the coachee to describe the desired goal or outcome precisely in positive terms.
- Make this sensory-specific evidence – what will they see, hear and feel when this is achieved?
- Make the goal SMART – Specific, Measurable, Achievable, Realistic, Timebound.

Reality

- Ask the coachee to describe what is the reality or current situation.
- Ask them how they currently perceive their performance in relation to their objective.
- Ask them if it helps to give themselves a benchmark – for example to rate themselves on a scale of 1 to 10 in terms of where they are now and where they want to be.

Options

- Ask the coachee to explore the situation or problem and to outline options for a solution. Encourage them not to have 'the solution' instantly.
- Encourage them to generate as many ideas for improvement as possible.
- Ask them, if there were a way for them to reach their objective, what would it be?

Will/Way Forward

- Ask the coachee to select idea(s) they will put in practice.
- Ask them what they will do, when and how.
- Discuss who else they need to involve in the actions and what resources are needed.
- Ask them to identify barriers they see to achieving the actions and how these can be overcome.

In order to give you an idea of the types of questions that can be asked in each phase of the GROW model, here are some suggestions:

Goal

Questions of the type that you can ask in the Goal section of the model encourage the coachee to set SMART, sensory-specific objectives for the coaching session:

- 'What is it you would like to discuss?'
- 'What would you like to achieve in this specific session?'

- 'What would you like to be different when you leave this session?'
- 'What would you be seeing, hearing or feeling that was different if you achieved your goal?'
- 'By when?'
- 'Is that realistic?'
- 'Can we do that in the time we have available? If not, how do you want to adjust your goal'?
- 'Will that be of real value to you?'

Reality

In the Reality phase of the GROW model, you ask questions to raise the coachee's awareness of what is currently happening:

- 'What is happening at the moment?'
- 'When is this an issue for you? At what times?'
- 'What do you notice when the issue occurs?'
- 'Apart from yourself, who else is involved?'
- 'What is their perception of the situation?'
- 'What other factors are relevant?'
- 'What actions have you tried so far to move you towards your goal?'

Options

During the Options phase of the model, you encourage the coachee to generate as many options as possible for changing the situation. They reinforce that all ideas are good ideas and they prompt creative thinking:

- 'What could you do to change the situation?'
- 'What alternatives are there to that approach?'
- 'What approach/actions have you seen used, or used yourself, in similar circumstances?'
- 'What would your best friend or your boss advise you to do?'
- 'Who might be able to help?'

Will/Way Forward

The fourth part of the model encourages the coachee to take responsibility for change. It narrows the options to those the coachee is most committed to and helps them create a plan of action to achieve their goal:

- 'Which options do you like the most?'
- 'Which options are you willing to carry out?'
- 'What are the next steps?'
- 'Precisely when will you take them?'
- 'What might get in the way?'
- 'If it did, how would you overcome this?'
- 'What support do you need?'
- 'How and when will you enlist that support?'

The GROW model remains the seminal model of coaching. It has also been adapted by some coaches, but, in essence, as you will see from the following alternative models, it lies at the heart of all effective coaching.

The STAR model

The STAR model of coaching again is future-focused. STAR is a mnemonic that stands for

- Situation
- Target
- Action
- Results or Review.

Using this four-step process you help the individual better understand the situation that they are in, the changes in behaviour they wish to make, how they will make these and when they will review them.

As in the GROW model, the coach uses a series of questions under each phase to raise awareness and to generate responsibility. Here are examples of the types of questions that can be used in each phase:

Situation

- 'What is the specific situation which is causing a difficulty for you?'
- 'What is happening now?'
- 'What are you doing now that is not having a positive impact?'
- 'What thoughts go through your mind and what do you and others say in the situation?'

Target

- 'What specifically would you like to be different? By when?'
- 'What thoughts would you like to be going through your mind and what would you like yourself and others to say?'
- 'What are your measures of success?'
- 'Are these achievable? If not, what would be and by when?'

Actions

- 'What actions can you take to change the situation?'
- 'What alternatives do you have?'
- 'What other options are there?'
- 'Which actions are most practicable?'
- 'How and by when?'
- 'How can you gain the support of others?'
- 'How and when can you do this?'

Results or Review

- 'What will be the results of your actions?'
- 'When will you review what you have done?'
- 'How do you want to feel as a result?'

The CIGAR model

The CIGAR approach evolved from the GROW and STAR models of coaching. This acronym stands for

- Current situation
- Ideal situation
- Gap between current situation and ideal situation
- Action planning
- Review.

Like both GROW and STAR, it helps the coachee discuss their current situation, set future-focused goals and then develop approaches to address the gap in performance.

Here are some examples of the questions that you can ask under each section of the model:

Current situation

- 'What is the context in which you are working?'
- 'What are the issues that you are facing?'
- 'Which issue gives you the biggest concern?'
- 'When does this issue occur?'
- 'Who is involved?'
- 'What are your thoughts on the reasons for this issue occurring?'

Ideal outcome

- 'What would be your ideal outcome to this issue?'
- 'When would you like this to happen?'

- 'How would you like this to happen?'
- 'Who, other than yourself, would be involved?'

Gap between current situation and ideal situation

- 'What is the gap between your ideal situation and the current situation?'
- 'On a scale of 1 (low) to 10 (high), where do you score the current situation?'
- 'On a scale of 1 (low) to 10 (high), where do you score the ideal situation?'

Action planning

- 'What actions will you take to bridge the gap between the current and ideal situation?'
- 'What are the first steps?'
- 'What is a milestone for you in terms of time?'
- 'What things may get in your way? If so, how will you overcome them?'
- 'What support do you need?'

Review

- 'How will you know if you have been successful?'
- 'When will you review your actions?'
- 'How will you celebrate success?'

The CLEAR model

Finally, CLEAR is a model for coaching that was developed by Peter Hawkins of the Bath Consulting Group.

It is different to the GROW, STAR and CIGAR models in that it places emphasis on the coaching relationship in terms of contracting and review. In this way the model promotes clarity regarding your role and how you can assist the coachee, as well as how effective you have been in relation to the contract.

CLEAR stands for:

- *Contracting* – agreeing the scope and outcome of the coaching, setting ground rules for working together.
- *Listening actively* and reflecting back the coachee's words so that they gain insights into the current situation.
- *Exploring* both the impact of the coachee's current behaviour and options for change.
- *Actions* – helping the coachee to develop a realistic plan of action for change.
- *Review* – reviewing the actions the coachee has taken as well as the effectiveness of the coaching relationship.

If you use the CLEAR framework, as a coach you ask questions of the following types:

Contracting

- 'What would you like to achieve from this coaching session?'
- 'What would you feel/hear/see differently as a result?'

- 'What is important to you in how we work together?'
- 'What role would you like me to take?'

Listening actively

- 'So what you are saying is ...'
- 'So to clarify, you think ...'
- 'To summarise ...'

Exploring

- 'Tell me more about what is happening now.'
- 'What effect does this have on you? On others?'
- 'What have you done already to try to change the situation?'
- 'What other alternative options do you have?'

Actions

- 'How can you change the situation?'
- 'What action will you take?'
- 'What steps are there in achieving the desired outcome?'
- 'When and how will you take them?'

Review

- 'So what actions have you taken?'
- 'What has been successful?'
- 'What barriers have you encountered?'

- 'What can you do to progress further?'
- 'How did you find working together?'
- 'What has worked well in our coaching partnership?'
- 'What could be improved?'

How to select a coaching model

The four coaching models that we have seen can each be used in a number of coaching situations. I do not advise switching between models. As you become more familiar and comfortable with coaching, you will find that you have a model that you favour.

Here are my perceptions on when it is particularly helpful to use each model:

- GROW: useful when someone starts a coaching conversation by articulating a clear goal.
- STAR: particularly useful during performance management discussions when an individual recognises they are not reaching a target.
- CIGAR: helpful when the coachee begins the conversation by giving lots of information about the context in which they are working.
- CLEAR: useful when coaching someone you do not know well as it includes setting ground rules for working together and finishes with a review.

If you are not familiar with coaching, I recommend that you begin the process by using the GROW or the CLEAR model as your framework. Both these models are ideal for following the coachee's agenda.

3: Models of Coaching

Summary

In this chapter I have outlined for you the history of coaching as well as four well-known models of coaching. The choice of which model you use needs to be situational. There is no one right way, not as long as the model that you use raises the coachee's awareness of their current situation and the options available for change, and helps them commit to a change. In the following chapters I explore the more specific skills needed in these key phases.

Questions to consider, having read this chapter, include:

- Which of the coaching models seemed to you the most relevant to your IT department?

- Which of the models are you committed to using?

- Of the four stages of the GROW model, the novice coach often misses out Reality and Options. Why do you think this is? What is the impact on the coachee of missing out these two stages?

CHAPTER 4: EFFECTIVE FEEDBACK

In this chapter I discuss:

- Coaching and the link to feedback.
- Beliefs about feedback.
- Tips for giving motivational and developmental feedback.
- Two models for giving feedback.
- How to deal with reactions to feedback.
- How to test and practise your skills for giving feedback.

Coaching and the link to feedback

Coaching to create high performance is underpinned by the ability to give effective feedback. Typically a coaching need is unearthed when a manager provides feedback on performance to their team member, or as result of feedback that others have provided to the coachee.

So, what is feedback?

A definition which is helpful is 'feedback is a communication to a person which gives them information about their performance, their behaviour and its impact on others'.

Giving feedback provides you the opportunity to

- be honest with your colleagues about their behaviour and performance,

- recognise them as individuals,
- identify what needs to be improved,
- create an opportunity for coaching to help them improve and
- help others realise their potential.

Feedback can help the individual to grow. It adds a further dimension to what you know about yourself and the public front that we display. Our public front is what we recognise in ourselves as well as what others see.

However, sometimes people will see you differently from the way you see yourself and you may be unaware of this. Sometimes you may be displaying emotions or behaviour that impact negatively on the group around you, but you are unaware of that. Feedback illuminates the blind spots we all have about ourselves and increases our self-awareness. Feedback helps increase our self-awareness and thereby opens areas which we can potentially capitalise on, improve and develop.

Beliefs about feedback

Fundamental to being able to give effective feedback is the belief that feedback is a helpful, healthy and positive communication between two people. As we have seen, the purpose of feedback is to maintain and improve performance – it should therefore have both a positive intention and impact. Consequently it is vital that the whole feedback process, whether giving motivational feedback (on what has gone well) or developmental feedback (on where the individual can improve) is conducted in a positive and constructive way.

4: Effective Feedback

There are two types of feedback that you can give and receive: motivational feedback and developmental feedback. Motivational feedback centres around praise – what the individual is doing well, what you as their manager would like them to continue, their strengths. Providing motivational feedback boosts an individual's confidence when the words are sincere and well meant. It encourages them to continue demonstrating behaviours which are their strengths.

Developmental feedback centres around areas for improvement and development – what the individual could do better. You will notice that I have used the term 'developmental feedback', not 'criticism' or 'constructive feedback', as the intention is to help the individual to improve. All feedback should be constructive and if you start a feedback session by using words such as 'criticism', the impact will be that the individual regards the session as such!

Providing feedback on performance should be a regular part of a manager's role. Like coaching itself, it should have a positive intent: to improve performance and to keep people on track. So why do many managers, not just in IT, but everywhere, neglect this important skill or leave it to the once-yearly performance review?

I have found that, in practice, managers often shy away from both giving and asking for feedback. Below are some of the possible reasons.

Some people hold back from giving motivational feedback because:

- They think that compliments are inappropriate, because the staff member is only doing what they are paid to do.

- They feel too embarrassed.
- They believe that the person receiving the feedback may relax and take it easy.
- They believe that the person receiving the feedback may be suspicious of their motives.
- They think that the feedback may be misinterpreted as a ploy to fish for compliments in return.
- They don't like receiving motivational feedback themselves.

Some people hold back from giving developmental feedback because:

- They worry that they might upset the receiver.
- They are concerned that the receiver may reject them or reject the feedback.
- They are concerned that the person might retaliate with developmental feedback themselves.
- They are concerned that it may end in a confrontation that would be difficult to resolve and might damage future relations.
- They think that the issue is too trivial, and that it would be better saved up for something more substantial.
- They don't like receiving developmental feedback themselves.

Do any of the above reasons strike a chord with you?

Ten tips for giving effective motivational and developmental feedback

So, how should you provide feedback? Do remember to consider the receiver when you provide feedback. Most of us prefer feedback to be given in private and as soon after the event as possible. Feedback can be written or spoken and mostly the latter is more powerful. Here are 10 tips for giving effective feedback:

- Prioritise your feedback – don't overload the receiver. It is better to provide feedback on two to three points, rather than on 30 which are then more likely to be forgotten.

- Give feedback on observed behaviour – what the individual has said or done; don't make subjective judgements. It is better to say, 'I noticed that you did not contact the sponsor last week', rather than, 'I think you can't be bothered to make contact with the sponsor'.

- Be specific – use examples, don't make generalisations. It is more effective to say 'I really liked the way the report was laid out clearly' than 'well done for the report'.

- Give motivational feedback before developmental – don't start on a negative when you have a positive to offer too.

- Do separate motivational from developmental feedback – do not link the two with 'but' or 'however' as this negates what has gone before.

- Be clear about what the individual did well and what they could do to improve.

- Ask questions when giving feedback – don't make the conversation one-sided; ask the individual what they think they did well, where they think they can improve.

- Time your feedback – say it while it is fresh, don't wait till a long time after the event.

- When providing feedback, own it; make it personal to you – unless you are using 360° feedback as part of the coaching session, best practice is to feed back on behaviour which you have personally observed and not on that which has been reported to you by someone else.

- Have a positive intention when you give feedback – don't use feedback to 'get at someone'; the purpose of feedback is to help the individual.

Two feedback frameworks

Here are two frameworks for giving feedback that represent best practice. The first is called MADASA. This focuses on inviting the individual to self-assess. The benefit of this approach is that the feedback session becomes a two-way dialogue. Often individuals know themselves what they have done well and where they can improve.

Here is the MADASA model:

Motivational feedback

In order to start positively and to encourage the individual to self-assess, ask the individual to provide themselves with motivational feedback by asking, 'What did you do well?'

Add your motivational feedback

Examples include, 'What I saw/heard/liked was ...', or 'What I noticed which had a positive effect was ...'.

Developmental feedback

Ask the individual, 'What could you improve or do differently?'

Add your developmental feedback

Examples include, 'What I noticed was ...' or 'What I did not see/hear was ...'

Seek suggestions

Ask the individual, 'What action could you take to improve this?'

Add your suggestions: 'What I suggest that you do differently next time is ...'.

Agree next steps

Ask the individual, 'So we are both clear, what have we agreed as the next steps?'

AID Model

The second framework is called AID. You can use this to feed back what you have observed as well as the impact of the person's behaviour and your advice.

Action

What was done or said, what was not done or not said:

- 'What I noticed was ...'
- 'What I saw was ...'
- 'When you didn't say/didn't do ...'

Impact

What impact or effect the person's behaviour had (on the task, procedure, climate or individual):

- 'It had the effect of ...'
- 'It caused ...'
- 'The impact/effect on me/the task/the process was ...'
- 'It made me feel ...'

Do

What could be done more (motivational), what could be done differently (developmental):

- 'I'd encourage you to do/say that more often.'
- 'I'd encourage you to continue to do/say that.'
- 'What I would have liked ...'
- 'What I would encourage you to do next time is ...'
- 'What I suggest you do differently is ...'

Both MADASA and AID can be combined. So, in the sections of MADASA when you are providing feedback, my suggestion is that you use the AID framework to help you.

Ideas to prepare the recipient for feedback that will be given

When delivering feedback, the giver needs to be conscious of the reactions of the receiver. Ideally people should be receptive to feedback and see it as helpful. In order to ensure that they understand the feedback, they need to listen and avoid rejecting what has been said, arguing or being defensive. Asking questions to clarify matters fully and seeking examples are useful. The receiver of the feedback should also ideally acknowledge the giver and show their appreciation; the feedback may not have been easy to give.

This is the ideal. In reality a wide variety of reactions often occur. People may:

- deny what has happened – this reaction often accompanies the initial shock of feedback;
- show emotion – be upset, angry or go quiet as the message sinks in;
- justify their actions and find excuses for their behaviour.

These reactions can occur when given motivational feedback as well as developmental. For example:

An individual is told:

'I noticed you took responsibility for speaking to the sponsor about the issue, which meant they were able to give you their support on the matter. Well done'

The individual replies:

'Oh, it was nothing.' (Blushes.) 'It wasn't my idea really.'

As a coach you need to be prepared for and aware of potential reactions and take appropriate courses of action to help people accept feedback. Some tips are:

- If the recipient is in denial: reiterate the facts, what you saw or heard; postpone any further discussion until later.
- If the recipient of the feedback attempts justification: refer the individual to the standards expected of them; ask them what they could do differently to prevent the situation happening again.

Test your feedback skills

To help reinforce your effectiveness in giving feedback, look at what was said by an IT manager during the following feedback discussions and assess whether this is good or bad practice. You will find the ideal answers at the end of this chapter.

- 'I've heard from some of the team that they're unhappy with the way you're behaving towards them.'
- 'The way that you prepared the budget was very good. I liked the way all the elements were broken down. There was an error in one of the additions, but overall it was very good.'
- 'I could tell you didn't like him, you seemed really offhand.'
- 'Well done. I saw you arrive at 8.00 a.m. to finish the job in time. I did notice that you've had difficulty getting everyone's input. Next time you have a similar deadline, what do you think you could do differently?'
- 'Your presentation was very poor. There were spelling mistakes on the first 10 pages; there was no structure; I

didn't see a beginning, a middle or an end; your tone of voice was very monotonous; you did not make eye contact with the audience; and you finished abruptly and then you could not answer the question at the end.'

- 'The report is excellent. I like the fact that it is concise – only four pages long – which made it very easy for me to read.'

- 'I've noticed an improvement in the number of questions you are asking during the call; however, you still need to listen more actively'.

- 'Oh, Gavin, I forgot to mention, when I got last quarter's report a month or so ago, the first two pages were missing.'

- 'I'm fed up with having to play nursemaid to you lot. I can't rely on you for anything. Tom Butcher has just been on the phone again to say his e-mail facility is still not working!'

- 'So what did you think you did well in running the meeting?'

  o 'I was pleased with the way I was able to get everyone to have their say.'

  o 'Yes, I really liked the fact that you asked open questions. I heard you say to the group, "So what does everyone think?" after John had put forward his suggestion. You also encouraged the quieter members of the group to speak up. For example, you asked Lorna what else she wanted to add. What do you think you could do next time to improve the meeting?'

o 'Well, I suppose I could try to ensure that everyone knows what's been agreed – it was difficult at times to follow that.'

o 'Yes, I suggest that next time you consider appointing someone to take the notes as this will help you know what has been agreed.'

Practise your feedback

How effective are your feedback skills? The next time you provide feedback, ask the person to whom you gave feedback to rate it! The following form should help you to do this:

Did the person who gave you the feedback:	YES/NO
Ask you first what you thought you did well?	
Give specific examples of what they heard or saw you do?	
Describe the impact/effect of your behaviour/actions	
Give you encouragement to continue this behaviour?	
Ask you first what you thought you could have done differently?	
Give specific examples of what they heard or saw you do or not do?	

Describe the impact/effect of your behaviour/actions	
Suggest what they would like you to do differently next time?	

Table 4: Coaching skills checklist

Summary

Feedback can help a manager maintain and improve their team members' performance. It is an essential part of coaching. When well delivered, it can play an important part in creating a high-performance culture. My experience is that managers do benefit from receiving training in effective feedback skills in order to underpin their coaching. However, like any skill, unless you practise it regularly, it can become difficult to apply. I have encouraged you to be aware of people's reactions to feedback and to deal with them appropriately in order to support change.

Here are some questions to consider having read this chapter:

- What are the barriers you find to giving effective feedback?

- Consider the last feedback you gave someone. Did you use objective as well as specific language?

- What is the balance of motivational to developmental feedback that you provide?

- What reactions have you seen in others when they receive feedback and how have you managed these?

Answers

- 'I've heard from some of the team that they're unhappy with the way you're behaving towards them.'

This is poor feedback. Feedback should be based on what you personally have seen or heard.

- 'The way that you prepared the budget was very good; I liked the way all the elements were broken down. There was an error in one of the additions, but overall it was very good.'

Ouch! This was going so well until the giver of the feedback felt the need to say 'but overall it was very good.' This is an example of the old-fashioned sandwich technique which is no longer best practice. The impact of sandwiching developmental feedback between two pieces of motivational feedback is that the developmental feedback is forgotten by the receiver, who thinks everything is very good!

- 'I could tell you didn't like him, you seemed really off-hand.'

This is poor feedback. It is subjective and based on impressions.

- 'Well done. I saw you arrive at 8.00 a.m. to finish the job in time. I did notice that you've had difficulty getting everyone's input. Next time you have a similar deadline, what do you think you could do differently?'

This is effective feedback. It is objective and asks for the receiver's inputs.

- 'Your presentation was very poor. There were spelling mistakes on the first 10 pages; there was no structure; I didn't see a beginning, a middle or an end; your tone of voice was very monotonous; you did not make eye contact with the audience; and you finished abruptly and then you could not answer the question at the end.'

This is poor feedback. It is too long and the impact is very negative.

- 'The report is excellent. I like the fact that it is concise – only four pages long – which made it very easy for me to read.'

This is effective feedback. It is factual and outlines the effect or impact.

- 'I've noticed an improvement in the number of questions you are asking during the call; however, you still need to listen more actively.'

This is poor feedback. The giver starts the conversation well, but the 'however' detracts from the motivational feedback at the start of the conversation. This means that the receiver is more likely to hear the developmental rather than the motivational feedback.

- 'Oh, Gavin, I forgot to mention, when I got last quarter's report a month or so ago, the first two pages were missing.'

This is an example of poor feedback. Feedback should be given at or near to the event.

- 'I'm fed up with having to play nursemaid to you lot. I can't rely on you for anything. Tom Butcher has just been on the phone again to say his e-mail facility is still not working!'

This is poor feedback. Feedback given in anger does not have a positive intent!

- 'So what did you think you did well in running the meeting?'
  - ○ 'I was pleased with the way I was able to get everyone to have their say.'
  - ○ 'Yes, I really liked the fact that you asked open questions. I heard you say to the group, "So what does everyone think?" after John had put forward his suggestion. You also encouraged the quieter members of the group to speak up. For example, you asked Lorna what else she wanted to add. What do you think you could do next time to improve the meeting?'
  - ○ 'Well, I suppose I could try to ensure that everyone knows what's been agreed – it was difficult at times to follow that.'
  - ○ 'Yes, I suggest that next time you consider appointing someone to take the notes as this will help you know what has been agreed.'

This is effective feedback. There is a two-way dialogue.

CHAPTER 5: CONTRACTING AND GOAL-SETTING

In this chapter I provide guidance on:

- How to 'contract' with a coachee.
- How to set SMART goals with a coachee.
- The pitfalls when helping the coachee set goals.

The beginning of any coaching partnership is key to developing an ongoing relationship. I have supervised many coaches who have privately sought advice about coaching relationships that have gone wrong. Typically the problems they have encountered relate to the lack of clarity about how they will work with their coachee and the lack of agreed objectives for the coaching they are about to undertake.

Contracting with the coachee

At the beginning of any coaching relationship it is important to agree a set of ground rules for how you will work together with the coachee. Effective coaching is dependent on mutual respect, trust and understanding. It is helpful therefore to establish a set of ground rules with the coachee for how you will both work together. A 'contract' is another term for a working agreement. This sets out the boundaries that define what you and coachee can expect and not expect in working together. Coaching contracts set the tone for the coaching relationship. They serve as a reference point against which the coaching relationship can be evaluated as the coaching progresses.

This can include such factors as:

- confidentiality,
- roles and responsibilities,
- expectations of each other and
- how you will work together.

It is helpful to write down the ground rules and, if the coachee wants to, for both of you to sign them. Here is an example of a contract that one IT manager set with his coachee:

The coach agrees to:

Keep the contents of our coaching sessions confidential

Support and encourage you during the coaching sessions

Challenge your thinking by questioning and observation

Provide you with in-the-moment feedback on your observed behaviour

The coachee agrees to:

Keep to the time and dates set for the three coaching sessions

Write up the actions arising from each session

Take responsibility for implementing the actions

Review the actions taken at the start of each session

The benefits of starting the coaching process with a contract are that it lays the foundation of the coaching partnership and ensures that no assumptions are made by either side.

In addition to the topics outlined above, it is also helpful to set out where the coaching will take place, and how often and when progress and the working relationship will be reviewed.

Typically, at the contracting stage you will need to establish how many coaching sessions you will facilitate. This will very much depend on the coachee and their need. Some coaching can take place in one session. Sometimes coaching takes place over six. Typically three sessions are held, either face to face or on the telephone. Alternatively they can be a mixture of face to face and telephone calls.

We recommend that at the start of every coaching session, you not only identify what the coachee wants to achieve from the session, but also ask questions about your role; for example, 'how can I help you today?' A useful process to begin each coaching session therefore is to focus on:

- What exactly do you want to achieve from this coaching session?
- What do you want to leave with today?
- How do you want me to support you?
- How do you want me to be?

Setting SMART goals

The coaching journey begins by the coachee explaining where they are starting from and what is their final destination. Part of your role at the beginning of a coaching contract, and indeed as part of every session, is to define a well-formed outcome for the session. What do I mean by a well-formed outcome? This is a goal that is desirable, worthwhile and achievable by the coachee.

Whatever coaching model you decide to use, you will notice that goal-setting is a key component. The effective coach helps the coachee describe their goals in SMART terms. SMART is a behavioural approach to setting outcomes. It stands for Specific, Measurable, Achievable, Realistic and Timebound.

Specific

So the coachee, for example, says that they would like to improve their time management. It is helpful for you to then question the coachee about specifically what aspects of their time management they would like to improve. Probe to discover what being a 'better' time manager means to the coachee. This could mean, for example, being able to prioritise more effectively or being able to delegate tasks. Unless you help the coachee to be specific, neither party gains clarity on what it is that they are aiming to achieve.

Measurable

In addition you can help the coachee by encouraging them to set measurable targets. How will the coachee know when they have achieved the goal? If the coachee has difficulty in setting a measure (for example, if they want to improve their delegation skills, how do they quantify where they are now?), it is useful to ask a scalar question. 'On a scale of 1 to 10, where do you rate your delegation skills now?' 'Where on a scale of 1 to 10 would you like to be?'

It is useful when coaching to explore with the coachee what measures already exist to help them assess their current performance. For example, they may have access to 360° feedback; perhaps they have undertaken a diagnostic test such as Prism Personal Performance Mapping®

(*www.prism-profiling.com*) to help them better understand where they are now.

Achievable

It is important to check that the coachee (and you as the coach) believes that they can actually achieve this goal. It may be that you will have to help the coachee to break down a large goal into smaller, more achievable pieces. For example, if the coachee says that they want to be promoted to project manager, it could be that one of the first goals would be to obtain a Prince 2 qualification by March next year. By breaking a large goal down into bite-size chunks, the coachee is more likely to achieve their ultimate goal, and to feel better about what they are aiming to achieve.

Realistic

It is useful to ask the coachee, 'Is this a worthwhile goal?' If the goal is not a realistic one, for example if the coachee does not have the time or the resources to achieve the goal, the impact can be demoralising. The coachee is unlikely to move towards a positive outcome.

Timebound

Discuss with the coachee how long they believe it will take to achieve their goal. Setting a timescale provides a milestone for the coachee. It is helpful to question the coachee about how much time they have in reality and whether the time limits that they set themselves are truly realistic.

Which of these objectives is SMART?

During the coaching process, you need to recognise objectives that are SMART and those which are not. Look at the list below and decide which objectives are SMART. You will not be able to tell from this list whether the goal is achievable or realistic, but for the purpose of the exercise, please assume they are.

Check your answers at the end of this chapter.

- Take additional training on general issues.
- Reduce the project implementation costs by 31 December.
- Be more willing to make presentations.
- Learn to look back and consider the bigger picture.
- Gain understanding of the customer database.
- Continue to provide a first-class level of customer service.
- Hold a progress meeting with all the team in order to delegate work appropriately.
- Ensure that 80% of managers receive performance management training by 31 December this year.
- Achieve £100,000 of new business from new customers by 31 December this year.
- Increase my confidence when speaking to senior managers.

Pitfalls when helping the coachee to set goals

When helping the coachee to set SMART goals, here are some tips on things to watch out for:

- The coachee sets a goal in negative terms – for example, they say that their goal is to not be terrified when giving presentations.

Encourage the coachee to reframe their goal in positive language. This means that they might say, for example, that they want to be more confident when presenting. It is better to help the coachee focus on what they do want rather than what they don't.

- The coachee uses terms such as 'better' or 'more' when speaking about their goal. For example, they want to be a better manager or more skilful at managing stakeholders.

Ask the coachee to clarify what 'better' or 'more' means to them. Encourage them to be specific.

- The coachee sets a goal that is outside their control. For example, they want to change the culture in the organisation (and they are a member of staff).

Encourage the coachee to focus on a goal that they can realistically achieve and that is within their control.

- The coachee cannot describe a SMART goal.

Ask the coachee to visualise what they will see, hear, feel or do when they are achieving their goal. Help them to describe a future time that provides a mental picture of what they are trying to achieve; for example, 'What will you see, hear and feel?' 'What will you be thinking to yourself?' 'What will other people see or hear?'

What to do if the coachee does not know what they want to achieve or if there are too many goals

There may be occasions when the coachee is not sure of exactly what they want to achieve. Alternatively, they may have too many goals that they want to focus on. Here are two techniques that may help.

If the coachee does not know where to start, one useful technique is to ask them to depict their life–work balance.

Draw a circle and divide this into segments. Ask the coachee to imagine that each segment represents an aspect of their life and work. For example, one segment could represent family and friends, another financial stability, another well-being, another career progression, etc. Invite the coachee to label the segments as they see fit; there are no rights or wrongs.

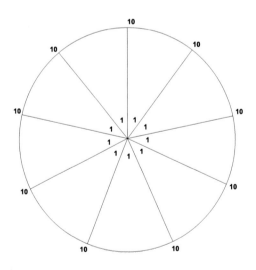

Figure 3: Balance wheel

Next, ask the coachee to assign a scale of 1 to 10 to each segment of the wheel, where 1 is highly dissatisfied and 10 is highly satisfied. Ask them to rate their satisfaction level with each of the segments. Emphasise that there are no rights or wrongs. Then, depending on where the coachee scores lowest, ask them to identify a goal for improvement that is realistic, achievable and worthwhile to them.

You can use the balance wheel to help drive an objective on any topic. So, for example, if someone says that they want to improve their time management, you could ask them to use the wheel to describe the different segments of time management. This could be, for example:

* planning,
* prioritisation,
* dealing with time-wasters,
* managing interruptions,
* delegation,
* using peak energy time.

Again, for each of the segments that the coachee describes, ask them to give it a score out of 10. In this way you will be able to help the coachee identify their strengths and areas for development.

A key point here is that the lowest scores that a coachee gives may not be the area in which they set their goal. Check with the coachee that they are comfortable with this and that the outcome they desire is worth the energy and time it will take to achieve.

If, on the other hand, the coachee has many goals that they want to achieve, a useful technique is to ask them to set out the advantages of achieving each of them. Discuss with them the benefits they will receive from each and what will happen as a result.

Next, encourage the coachee to prioritise their goals. Ask questions around what would be valuable to them to achieve during this particular coaching session, for example:

- 'What would be valuable for you to gain from this session?'
- 'What would make this session worthwhile for you?'
- 'At the end of this session, what do you want to walk away with?'
- 'Which of these goals is more important to you?'
- 'What is the priority outcome for you right now?'

Summary

In this chapter I have outlined for you the importance of establishing ground rules and goals at the start of a coaching relationship. In particular I have focused on the practicalities of how to 'contract' with a coachee. I have also discussed the need to help the coachee with setting SMART goals and using sensory-specific visualisation and techniques such as prioritisation and the balance wheel to help identify specific goals. In the next chapters I provide you with guidance on listening and questioning skills during coaching, generating options and encouraging change.

Here are some questions to consider having read this chapter:

- When you are running your next coaching session, what would you propose to the coachee as part of the coaching contract/ground rules for working together?
- What assessment tools do you have access to in your organisation that could help the coachee provide a picture of their performance?
- What is the shape of your own balance wheel? Set yourself a personal goal as a result of completing the wheel. Make sure that this is goal is SMART.

Answers

I have listed below the answers to whether the example objectives are SMART or not:

- Take additional training on general issues.

No. Not specific enough. What is general training? No timeframe set.

- Reduce the project implementation costs by 31 December.

No. How much should the cost of photocopying be reduced by?

- Be more willing to make presentations.

No. Not specific, measurable or timebound.

- Learn to look back and consider the bigger picture.

No. Not specific, measurable or timebound.

- Gain understanding of the customer database.

No. Not specific, measurable or timebound.

- Continue to provide a first-class level of customer service.

No. Not specific, measurable or timebound.

- Hold a progress meeting with all the team in order to delegate work appropriately.

No. Not specific, measurable or timebound.

- Ensure that 80% of managers receive performance management training by 31 December this year.

Yes. Specific, measurable and timebound.

- Achieve £100,000 of new business from new customers by 31 December this year.

Yes. Specific, measurable and timebound.

- Increase my confidence when speaking to senior managers.

No. Not specific, measurable or timebound.

CHAPTER 6: LISTENING AND QUESTIONING SKILLS

Skilful questioning and active listening are the two foundation blocks of coaching. In this chapter I aim to help you improve your listening and questioning skills by introducing:

* The art of listening in a coaching environment.
* Powerful questions and how to use them effectively to coach.
* Bad behaviours to avoid.

Active listening

I have often been surprised by the amount of people that I coach who tell me that one of the things they value most from coaching is being heard. Often we hurry through life without having the opportunity to properly express ourselves and to be acknowledged and heard. In the workplace, especially in an IT environment, the focus of most managers' attention is on processes and systems. Therefore being listened to can be a new and enlightening experience for many IT professionals. One of the key skills of the coach is to be able to actively listen.

When coachees feel that they are truly listened to, it is a powerful experience which encourages personal introspection and reflection. They feel more confident, learn more about themselves and are more receptive to change.

What does this mean in practice for you?

6: Listening and Questioning Skills

Below is a list of the attributes of good and bad coaches. Consider each statement in turn and decide whether you agree or disagree that these are the behaviours that effective coaches demonstrate:

Effective coaches:	Agree/Disagree
1. Listen to content	
2. Try to really understand, getting the full meaning	
3. Spend time when listening getting ready to talk	
4. Allow themselves to daydream	
5. Do one thing at a time – listen	
6. Ask for confirmation if required	
7. Question when necessary	
8. Use silence to show they are listening	
9. Listen for main ideas	
10. Control their emotions	
11. Listen for facts, themes and impressions	
12. Concentrate; fight distractions	

13. Divide their attention or try to do something else	
14. Pay particular attention to emotional words	
15. Keep an open mind	
16. Want people to 'get on with it'	
17. Check understanding	
18. Take a part-meaning from the conversation	
19. Maintain patience and concentration	
20. Nod and make eye contact	
21. Summarise key points using the coachee's language	
22. Summarise key points in their own words	
23. Use unresponsive body language	
24. Listen to style, e.g. grammar	

Table 5: Listening skills

You can find my suggested answers at the end of this chapter.

Good listening is therefore a major skill in coaching. As a coach you need to hear what is being said, what is the meaning of the words, as well as hearing what is not being said. You have to reflect back the coachee's words and show that you have heard what the coachee feels strongly about and why they feel strongly about it.

So why is this hard to demonstrate as a coach? Have you experienced any of these? How does it feel?

- Not listening – someone physically present but preoccupied shuffling papers, etc.
- Pretending to listen – the listener smiles and nods but in all the wrong places.
- Selective listening – the other person listens well but only to the parts in which they are interested.

Active listening is demanding of both time and energy. We need to focus on the coachee and be genuinely attentive and accepting of them. There is a saying that we have two ears and one mouth and we should use them in that proportion. Yet typically, as we start listening to others, our own inner dialogue begins to kick in. 'I've been in that same situation too', 'I hope he gets to the point quickly', 'I wonder what time I'll get home today.' Our inner voice begins to play in our head and, if we are not careful, it interferes with our ability to listen to others as we are so busy listening to ourselves.

Our inner dialogue

Everyone has an inner dialogue that runs through their head. It is a way of protecting ourselves and has a positive intention to be helpful. Yet our inner dialogue can stop us 'being in the moment' and focusing on others. It's the voice that tells us we 'must' or 'should' do something. It is part of the inner self that wants to communicate a message such as 'take care', 'be cautious', 'don't do this'.

Inner dialogue can also have a negative impact both on you as the coach and on the coachee. For us as the coach it can undermine confidence and distract us from listening. As a coachee, inner dialogue can prove restrictive and serve as a barrier to growth. Our inner voice tells us 'should' or 'can't' or 'try'. Telling ourselves these messages gives us barriers to acting with confidence and embracing change.

So, the first rule of active listening is to minimise our inner dialogue. Truly actively listening means switching off our inner voice and focusing on what the other person is saying. This means that we are on the same wavelength and that there is minimal interference.

Interference

Our inner dialogue can therefore interfere with our ability to listen effectively. It can also make us judgemental during a coaching session. Typical signs of judgemental rather than non-judgemental listening which should be avoided are:

Expressing an opinion or judgement

Where you express an opinion about the situation that the coachee is describing or pass a judgement: 'Well, if you ask me, you should have seen that coming.'

Evaluating the situation that the coachee has described

This could sound something like, 'Well, I don't think it's as bad as you make it out to be.'

Telling the coachee what to do

This involves being directive to the coachee: 'You should go and speak to him.'

Brushing aside what the coachee has said

Here you dismiss what the coachee has expressed; for example, 'Well, I'm sure it's not as bad as that.'

Making light of what the coachee has said

This could be by saying something such as, 'Oh, that doesn't sound as awful as you make out.'

Talking about yourself

Instead of listening and focusing on the coachee, you relate the topic to yourself and start talking about your own experiences; for example, 'Yes, I know. When I worked for Roger I found that the only way ...'

Using inappropriate humour

This is where you attempt to make light of the situation via ill-judged humour.

Admonishing the coachee

You use expressions such as, 'How could you!' or 'You made a real fool of yourself.'

Giving advice

You provide advice to the coachee: 'If I were you ...' or 'What you need to do is ...'

Contradicting what the coachee is saying

You contradict what the coachee has said by such expressions as, 'I think that you are wrong there' or 'No, I disagree.'

The impact of any of these types of comment or intervention is that you appear judgemental. You lose your neutrality and the coaching session follows your agenda, not the coachee's.

So how do you stop this interference, particularly when your inner dialogue may be saying these things to you?

Three levels of listening

In their book *Co-active Coaching: New Skills for Coaching People Toward Success in Work and Life* (2007), Laura Whitworth, Henry Kimsey-House, Karen Kimsey-House and Phil Sandahl talk about three levels of listening that we use as coaches:

Level 1 listening is where you listen to your own internal dialogue and what it is telling you when you hear the coachee speak. This is the type of listening that potentially causes us to pass judgement and to follow our own agenda rather than that of the coachee, so we should use it least.

Level 2 listening is where you are focused on the coachee. You give them your undivided attention and are acutely aware of what they are saying. In level 2 listening you summarise and reflect back what the coachee has said. You are like a magic mirror that holds itself up to the coachee and echoes the coachee's words.

Level 3 listening is a deeper level of listening. It is about being tuned to the coachee's words and how they are saying them; to the tone of their voice; to their pauses, pitch, breathing, body language and energy. It is about picking up what is not being said as much as what is said.

Paraphrasing and reflecting back

To demonstrate level 2 and level 3 listening, you can use a variety of techniques such as:

- Summarising clearly and simply what has been said: 'So what you are saying is ...'

- Paraphrasing using the coachee's own words: 'So you have a lot of attachment, as you put it, to that way of working.'

- Getting to the heart of what the coachee is saying: 'So if I understand you correctly, the key issue for you is ...'

- Reflecting the coachee's feelings: 'It sounds as though ...' or ' It seems that ...'

- Encouraging the coachee to explore possibilities: 'I'm wondering what is an option for you in that situation?'

- Clarifying when they are not sure: 'You said you have no contact with him on a regular basis, why do you think this is important?'

- Balancing the different elements of what the coachee has said: 'So on the one hand it seems that *xx*, and on the other you are saying *yy*.'
- Reflecting the energy the coachee has expressed around a topic: 'I can hear through your tone of voice that there is a lot of frustration there.'
- Pointing out habits or patterns of behaviour: 'You have talked a lot about having difficulties now and in the past delegating to other people, is this a pattern of behaviour for you?'

Above all, active listening encourages you to raise your own awareness of the coachee currently is in any given situation and what the options are for their future action. Coupled with effective questioning, active listening is an invaluable way of helping the coachee achieve their goal.

Question types

Active listening is the bridge to effective questioning in a coaching session. In order to use effectively questions during a coaching session, you need first to have listened to what the coachee is saying. You also need to understand the range of question types that can be used by the coach. Here is a description of the different question types and their advantages.

Closed questions

A closed question is one that can be answered 'yes' or 'no', for example:

- 'Did you sleep well last night?'

- 'Did you have a good weekend?'
- 'Have you finished the schedules for next week?'
- 'Are you happy to take on that role?'

Advantages of closed questions

- They put the person at ease at the initial stages of the conversation.
- They put you in control of the situation.
- They help to obtain specific facts quickly.
- They are useful for 'testing understanding' and 'summarising'.
- They allow you to get agreement.

Open questions

An open question allows you to receive more information than a closed question. Open questions start with what, why, how, when, which or who. They can also use the words 'tell', 'describe' and 'explain', for example:

- 'Tell me more about what happened.'
- 'What are your personal views on this idea?'
- 'How do you think that might work in reality?'
- 'Explain exactly what happened when you saw him.'

Open questions also allow you to probe for more information. Probing questions are a type of open question, for example:

- 'What would be the outcome if you did that?'
- 'Why do you say that?'

- 'What makes you believe that would happen?'
- 'How do you mean?'

Advantages of open questions

- They are useful to establish all the facts.
- They allow people to express their views.
- They build rapport and show you are interested.
- Probing questions allow you to clarify your understanding.

Limiting questions

A limiting question is one that gives the recipient a choice, for example:

- 'What would you like to do first – answer your e-mails or make the calls?'

Advantages of limiting questions

- Useful to gain agreement and when time is short.

Leading questions

A leading question is when the answer is in the question, for example:

- 'You are going to send out those tickets today, aren't you?'

Advantage of leading questions

- Useful for gaining clarity and understanding.

So, having read the descriptions, look at the following questions and decide whether each one is an example of open, probing, closed, limiting or leading question types.

Question	Question type
How can we get this done?	
What made you say that?	
You do want to go today, don't you?	
Do you want to pay by cheque or by credit card?	
Shall I post it to you?	
I'll come back to you later today. Is that OK?	
Shall I wrap it for you or would you like to do it?	
What reasons did he give for not turning up?	
You said you had some experience, when did you work in this area?	
Who is the best person to speak to?	

Where is the carpet department?	
You said you were unhappy, why was that?	
You have got your money with you, haven't you?	
Would you like tea or coffee?	
Tell me why you selected this one	
We will go together, won't we?	
Have you the correct change?	
Is your name Sylvia?	
Is it red or green?	
You will do that for me, won't you?	

Table 6: Question types

You can compare your answers with the ones at the end of the chapter.

You'll have probably guessed by now that open questions are the most useful during a coaching session. Open questions lead to exploration and options; they open up possibilities and encourage responsibility. The problem is that the brain is wired to ask more closed questions than open. Closed questions relate to our need for closure, for one answer, to be right. Remember, therefore, that to get the most from the coaching session, you need to ask open questions. But the session should not be an inquisition. It is important to listen as well as to question. Remember also to let your questions land. Do not be afraid of silence or feel that you have to answer the question for the coachee. A question type to avoid, especially at the beginning of a coaching discussion, is 'why'. This can appear to be undermining the coachee and does not help develop trust and rapport during a coaching session.

When questioning, less is more. Here are some examples of what I call prompt questions. They are brief, open questions that encourage the coachee to think for themselves and come to their own conclusions.

- 'Where do you want to start?'
- 'Where are you now?'
- 'What do you think?'
- 'How can you move this forward?'
- 'Where do you want to go from here?'
- 'What's next?'
- 'What did you learn?'
- 'What will you do?'
- 'And now?'
- 'And?'

Powerful questions

In any coaching conversation there are going to be questions which are more powerful and resonate with the coachee more than others. Typically you can see when the question has made the coachee stop and think as they will pause or say, 'That's a good question'.

Powerful questions can be as simple as, 'So what's happening to you right now?' or 'So what's stopping you?' Typically you use level 3 listening to reflect back what you are hearing and pose a question. Powerful questions are contextual, but they can be as simple as

- 'It's almost as if you believe ...'
- 'It sounds as if you really want to ...'
- 'I'm wondering how much of a pattern there is in this behaviour.'

Typically you will find yourself using powerful questions when the coachee discusses the context of their issue and/or when they are generating options. You will probably find yourself using several during a coaching session.

Powerful questions generate 'ah-ha' moments for the coachee, so use them with confidence. If your own inner dialogue is asking you a question about what the coachee is saying, this is a cue to be brave and pose a question to the coachee. It may not always make the coachee stop and think, but chances are it could resonate with the coachee and move them towards achieving their goal.

Summary

Active listening and effective questioning lie at the heart of coaching. By using these two techniques you will be able to follow the coachee's agenda. Using level 2 and level 3 listening skills means that you will be focused on the coachee. Open questions will help you create awareness and responsibility.

Here are some questions to ask and an activity and try in relation to listening and questioning skills:

- Which people or types of conversation do you find it most easy to listen to? What does this tell you about your listening skills?

- What is your inner dialogue telling you now? How can you learn to 'switch off' or 'turn down' your inner dialogue during a coaching session?

- Think of the last time that you asked people questions. What types of question were you using (open, closed, leading, limiting)?

- Formulate some open questions that you can use the next time that you hold a meeting with someone in the IT department. This will help you to practise in preparation for your next coaching session.

Answers

Effective coaches:	Agree/Disagree
1. Listen to content	Agree
2. Try to really understand, getting the full meaning	Agree
3. Spend time when listening getting ready to talk	Disagree
4. Allow themselves to daydream	Disagree
5. Do one thing at a time – listen	Agree
6. Ask for confirmation if required	Agree

7. Question when necessary	Agree
8. Use silence to show they are listening	Disagree
9. Listen for main ideas	Disagree
10. Control their emotions	Agree
11. Listen for facts, themes and impressions	Agree
12. Concentrate; fight distractions	Agree
13. Divide their attention or try to do something else	Disagree
14. Pay particular attention to emotional words	Disagree
15. Keep an open mind	Agree
16. Want people to 'get on with it'	Disagree
17. Check understanding	Agree
18. Take a part-meaning from the conversation	Disagree
19. Maintain patience and concentration	Agree
20. Nod and make eye contact	Agree
21. Summarise key points using the coachee's language	Agree
22. Summarise key points in their own words	Disagree

23. Use unresponsive body language	Disagree
24. Listen to style, e.g. grammar	Disagree

Table 7: Listening skills: answers

Question	Question type
How can we get this done?	Open
What made you say that?	Probing
You do want to go today, don't you?	Leading
Do you want to pay by cheque or by credit card?	Limiting
Shall I post it to you?	Closed
I'll come back to you later today. Is that OK?	Closed
Shall I wrap it for you or would you like to do it?	Limiting
What reasons did he give for not turning up?	Open
You said you had some experience, when did you work in this area?	Probing
Who is the best person to speak to?	Open
Where is the carpet department?	Open

You said you were unhappy, why was that?	Probing
You have got your money with you, haven't you?	Leading
Would you like tea or coffee?	Limiting
Tell me why you selected this one	Probing
We will go together, won't we?	Leading
Have you the correct change?	Closed
Is your name Sylvia?	Closed
Is it red or green?	Limiting
You will do that for me, won't you?	Leading

Table 8: Question types: answers

CHAPTER 7: GENERATING OPTIONS AND ENCOURAGING CHANGE

Questioning and listening will help you to get the best for the person you are coaching. As we have seen, coaching is a forward-focused activity.

In this chapter I will explore how you can help the individual

- Generate options for the future.
- Evaluate and select the approach(es) which will help them attain their goal.
- Create and implement a robust action plan.

I also provide exercises to help you consolidate and practise your own coaching skills.

Generating options for the future

I was in a coaching session recently that made me more aware than ever of how important it is in coaching to ensure that the coachee focuses forward on how to attain their goal, rather than remaining 'stuck' in the problem. The person I was coaching had recently been promoted within the IT department. They were suffering from a crisis of confidence in their new role. Having established a clear objective for the session and clarified my role as coach, we then discussed what was happening in the coachee's workplace currently. The coachee discussed the issues that they had with their immediate boss and other key stakeholders. The impact on the coachee was a loss in confidence. They were concerned that the reputation of the IT department was suffering under their leadership.

The coachee spoke at length about their issues and how they were affecting their behaviour. It seemed that the more they spoke about the situation, the more they were repeating themselves and going round in a circle. Having listened and reflected back to the coachee what I was hearing, it was clear that I needed to help the coachee move forward in order to help them rise above the current situation.

Forward-moving questions

In order to help the coachee attain their goal, as a coach you should encourage the individual to take action. Some people prefer to talk about their issues but are reluctant to take concrete steps to address them.

In order to move someone to action, it is helpful, once you have established and reflected back the current situation, to ask forward-moving questions. These are questions designed to help the coachee focus on the future, for example:

- 'So what next?'
- 'How can you resolve the issue?'
- 'What options do you have?'
- 'What do you want to do now?'
- 'What are your next steps?'
- 'What action arises out of this?'
- 'How can you move this forward?'
- 'Where do you want to take this?'

- 'What can you do differently?'
- 'What improvements can you make?'

Importantly, let the question hang. The temptation often is for you to provide an answer for the coachee. When we do this we are imposing our own thoughts and judgements on the individual. In order to coach effectively the coachee needs to take responsibility for their own actions. They will not do this if we take the role of adviser, trainer, teacher or parent.

Our natural desire is to help. Therefore it comes easy and naturally to make suggestions or to 'prompt' the coachee into a specific action by asking a leading question. 'So you do want to go on an assertiveness course?' may seem a helpful suggestion, but if it does not come from the coachee, the chances are that they will not be as committed to the action as if it came to themselves.

Brainstorming

It is helpful to encourage the coachee to explore as many options as possible for improvement. Do not add your own ideas, even if the coachee asks, 'What do you think'. It is more helpful to encourage them to suggest ideas.

Remind the coachee of the principles of brainstorming:

- there should be no criticism,
- freewheeling is encouraged,
- quantity of ideas, not quality, is the first requirement,
- everything should be written down, however apparently impractical,
- ideas should cross-fertilise others,

- all ideas should be evaluated and not rejected out of hand.

Encourage the individual to discuss their ideas. Ensure that you or they capture each idea on paper. It does not matter how they create the ideas. Some people like to Mind Map®, some use Post-it® notes.

Mind Mapping® is where the coachee takes a piece of paper and writes the topic area in a circle in the centre of the paper. They let their ideas flow freely and write them on the paper. They then join similar ideas by lines and build on these.

Using Post-it® notes, the coachee writes their ideas. They use one Post-it® per idea. If appropriate the coachee can then cluster them into groups of ideas. You can then encourage the coachee to sort the Post-it® notes into an order or pathway of action. This means that the coachee sorts what they have written and lays this out in a timeline. One useful technique is to physically put the Post-it® notes on the floor and invite the coachee to walk and talk you through the actions. This provides a clearer sense of time span and behaviours. The coachee can also physically look back at the action they have taken and forward to the next steps.

What to do if the coachee runs out of ideas or cannot think of any

The temptation if a coachee has no ideas, or can only think of a couple options, is to jump in as the coach and offer a suggestion. I recommend that you only do this as a last resort. Allow the coachee the time and space to think for themselves. If you do make suggestions, ask the coachee, 'Would you like me to make a suggestion.'

Before you do this, however, if at all, here are some techniques you can use to help the coachee come up with more ideas:

- Encourage weird and wacky 'off the wall' ideas. Anything goes! For example, 'What is the weirdest thing you could do?' 'What would you have to do not to achieve your goal?' Sometimes a weird idea can springboard in to a more plausible one.

- Ask the coachee what they have seen other people do who have been successful in the area.

- Ask what they have done to overcome a similar issue in the past.

- Invite the person to take a helicopter view of their situation. Ask them to say what the pilot of the helicopter would be telling them as they were looking down.

- Ask the coachee to use a metaphor or analogy to describe the current situation. For example, if their situation was a mode of transport, what would it be, what is surrounding it, where would it be going, what are its next moves?

- Ask the coachee what their best friend would advise them to do.

- Ask the coachee what their boss what advise them to do.

- Ask the coachee what they would do in the situation if they could wave a magic wand.

- Invite the coachee to think of one more idea, no matter how crazy.

You may be reading this list and thinking that some of these techniques sound impractical. The idea is to encourage the coachee to open up possibilities. At this stage there is no evaluation. What you are doing in your role is enabling the coachee to think of alternative approaches.

Make sure that you or preferably the coachee captures the ideas that they have generated.

Evaluating options

Once the coachee has generated their ideas, help them to evaluate these one by one.

Here are some approaches and questions that you can use to do this:

- Look at the list of ideas and consider the advantages and disadvantages of each.
- What are the pros and cons of each idea?
- Which ideas take you furthest towards your goal?
- Give each idea a rating on a scale of 1 to 10 in terms of your commitment to turning the idea into action, where 1 = low and 10 = high.
- Prioritise the ideas in terms of their practicality and applicability in your mind.

Your role at this stage of the coaching is to encourage the coachee to evaluate all the options, not to reject them out of hand.

Action planning

In this phase of the coaching session, the coachee has generated and evaluated their options. Now you need to encourage them to commit to action.

Here are some prompt questions that you can use to do this:

- 'Which idea(s) will you take forward?'
- 'When will you do this?'
- 'How exactly will you do this?'
- 'What are the precise steps in the process?'
- 'What help or support do you need?'
- 'Who do you need to inform of your actions?'
- 'When will you do so?'

Further questions that are useful to ask at this stage centre around helping the coachee to overcome any potential blockages to action by thinking these through. Prompt the coachee to consider:

- 'What else might you need to consider when undertaking this action?'
- 'What could get in the way?'
- 'If it did, what can you do to overcome this?'

By thinking about potential barriers, the coachee may identify other actions that they need to take.

In addition it is helpful at this stage to check the coachee's commitment to the action they intend to take. You can ask questions such as:

- 'So where are you now?'
- 'What key thing will you take away from this session?'

- 'On a scale of 1 (low) to 10 (high) how committed are you to this action?'

Reviewing the actions

And don't forget to ask the coachee how and when they would like to review their actions. The coachee is far more likely to follow the action to its completion if they have a review point.

Remember not to force a review date on the coachee. Agree a time which is realistic to them. Offer your support and encouragement where appropriate.

Some further tips are to encourage the coachee to write down their actions and, where appropriate, to send you a copy. One school of thought is that you should write up the session. However, if you wish the coachee to take responsibility for their actions, the best process is to encourage them to own the writing up.

You both then have a copy of the discussion and action points to review at the start of the next coaching session. However, to reiterate, not all coaching needs to be done on a formal basis. You can use the same principles that we have described in a ten-minute chat at the water fountain, or in a fifteen-minute discussion on the phone.

Consolidating your skills

In the last section in this chapter, I would like to offer you the opportunity of consolidating your skills. Having learned about the practice of coaching, here are several exercises to help consolidate your learning. They consist of quizzes and exercises that allow you to reflect on what you have learned. They also contain several checklists that you can use to gain feedback during a coaching session.

The answers to the quizzes and exercises are contained at the end of this chapter.

The skills of coaching

Use this exercise to remind you of the skills of the effective coach. Read the following statements and identify which approaches an effective coach would use:

At the beginning of the coaching session

1a) 'What you need to do is improve your influencing skills.'

1b) 'I understand that you want to improve your influencing skills, is that correct?'

1c) 'What would you like to achieve from this session?'

2a) 'What makes you think that you can't influence effectively now?'

2b) 'What specific aspects of your influencing skills do you want to improve?'

2c) 'I can see why you might have problems in this area.'

3a) 'What's happening now when you try to influence people?'

3b) 'What approaches have you tried in the past?'

3c) 'When was the last time you failed to influence someone?'

7: Generating Options and Encouraging Change

During the coaching session

4a) 'What I suggest you do, then, is be less forceful in your views.'

4b) 'How do you think you can improve your influencing skills?'

4c) 'I had the same problem and in my experience it's best to listen more and talk less.'

5a) 'What options have you got?'

5b) 'Who do you think is an effective influencer in the media, what do you think they do?'

5c) 'What other routes might there be to improving?'

6a) 'Which option seems most achievable?'

6b) 'You need to start doing something about this straight away.'

6c) 'In my opinion, the only way to do it is to talk to her in person.'

At the end of coaching session

7a) 'What are you going to do going forward?'

7b) 'What are the next steps for you?'

7c) 'When you speak to her you need to tell her exactly how you feel.'

8a) 'When will you take this action?'

8b) 'What's wrong with seeing her this week?'

8c) 'I suggest that you see her this week.'

9a) 'What support do you need in achieving this?'

9b) 'When will you know if you've been successful?'

9c) 'Come back to me as soon as you've seen her and let me know the outcome.'

Phrases to use during the coaching session

Listed below are six situations when you can use open questions as a coach to manage the coaching session. List two or three OPEN questions under each category that you may potentially use:

Contracting with the coachee

Setting a goal for the coaching session

Exploring the current situation

Encouraging the coachee to generate options for action

Action planning

Reviewing actions taken

NB We encourage you to look back over the previous chapters to find examples of questions if you get stuck.

Coaching styles

Remind yourself of the three styles of coaching and when they are appropriate by reading the descriptions below. Complete the sections about when each style would work well.

Directing coaching style

- You retain control.
- You set objectives with the coachee, provide solutions and give clear and detailed instructions on what to do.
- You work closely with the coachee in implementing the solution, checking their understanding and giving feedback on progress.

A directing coaching style works well when:

Guiding coaching style

- You retain some control, but allow the coachee as much freedom as they feel comfortable with.
- You set objectives with the coachee, and discuss and explore issues with the coachee.
- You help the coachee to evaluate options for development. You add your suggestion as one of those options.
- You tend to only get involved with the coachee at their request.

A guiding coaching style will work well if:

Empowering coaching style

- You help the coachee to manage their own learning.
- You will typically use questions to help the coachee think things through for themselves.
- You encourage the coachee to develop their own solutions and ways forward.
- You act as a sounding board for coachees and review their experiences with them.

An empowering coaching style will work well if:

See the end of this chapter for potential answers.

Active listening exercise

To improve your level 2 and level 3 listening, practise listening with a partner.

Specifically paraphrase what they have said. Repeat back their own words where possible. Listen for the energy in their voice and observe their body language. Reflect back what you see using phrases such as 'I'm wondering if ...' to access level 3 listening.

Your skills as a coach

Use this checklist to either self-assess your skills or to gain feedback about your skills during or after a coaching session.

Skill	How you can do this
1. Ensure SMART objectives are set	Use questioning to help coachee set SMART/sensory-specific evidence objectives for the session
2. Ensure you are clear about the role you can play as coach	Question the coachee around the role you can play in the session
3. Build and maintain rapport	Ensure a high level of rapport, e.g. matching body language, voice tone, speed, words and phrases
4. Increase the coachee's awareness of the current situation	Use questions to enable coachee to gain increased awareness of current performance level

5. Follow the coachee's lead	Demonstrate flexibility to follow the lead or interest of the coachee
6. Actively listen	Demonstrate active listening through summarising, checking understanding, and non-verbal behaviour
8. Question rather than tell	Use a predominantly questioning style
9. Use open questions	Use predominantly open and probing questions
10. Help the coachee explore options	Encourage the coachee to consider alternatives, do not suggest your own options
11. Encourage the coachee to specify exact next steps	Question the coachee to help them set a specific action plan with timescales, and gain their commitment

Table 9: Your skills as a coach

GROW observation sheet

Ask someone to observe you during a coaching session, with the coachee's permission. Invite the observer to write observations and examples of what you are saying during each phase of the GROW model.

| Observation feedback on: _____ ||
Coaching process	**Observations and examples**
G What GOALS were established? List the questions the coach asked	
R How was the REALITY explored? List the questions the coach asked	
O What OPTIONS were discussed? List the questions the coach asked	
W How was WILL/WAY FORWARD arrived at? List the questions the coach asked	

Table 10: Coaching observation sheet

Summary

In this chapter I have outlined techniques for you to use to help the coachee move towards their goal. These include generating options for the future and evaluating and selecting the approach(es) which will help them attain their goal. I have also outlined how you can help the coachee to create a robust action plan. Finally in this chapter I have provided you with checklists and exercises to help you embed the skills that you have learned.

Here are some questions to ask yourself in relation to this chapter:

- What techniques are you aware of that you can use to encourage the coachee to generate options for change?
- Think of a time when you have changed a behaviour or learned a new skill. What encouraged you to do this? How can you use this insight when you are coaching?
- What are the key learning points for you about coaching?
- What do you need to remember to do at your next coaching session?

Answers

Coaching skills

At the beginning of the coaching session

1c) What would you like to achieve from this session?

7: Generating Options and Encouraging Change

The objectives of the session should be driven by the coachee, not the coach.

2b) What specific aspects of your influencing skills do you want to improve?

The coachee's objectives should be as specific as possible.

3a) What's happening now when you try to influence people?

3b) What approaches have you tried in the past?

A discussion should take place around the coachee's current and past approaches to the situation. The language used by the coach should be positive, not, for example, 'failed to influence'.

During the coaching session

4b) How do you think you can improve your influencing skills?

You should encourage the coachee to think of their own solutions.

5a) What options have you got?

5c) What other routes might there be to improving?

The coach should encourage the coachee to explore all options.

6a) Which option seems most achievable?

The coach should help the coachee select the options that seem most realistic and achievable to them.

7: Generating Options and Encouraging Change

At the end of coaching session

7a) What are you going to do going forward?

7b) What are the next steps for you?

The coachee needs to determine and be committed to the action.

8a) When will you take this action?

The coach should encourage the coachee to set their own timescales.

9a) What support do you need in achieving this?

9b) When will you know if you've been successful?

You should help the coachee determine the support they need and the criteria for success. These should not be imposed by you.

Coaching styles

A directing coaching style works well when:

- The coachee lacks confidence and competence.
- They are new to the job or task and have no experience in this area.
- They are new to the role and have no previous experience in this area.

A guiding coaching style works well when:

- The coachee lacks competence but is confident.
- The coachee lacks confidence but is competent.
- The coachee has not undertaken the specific task before, but may have experience of similar tasks.

- The coachee has not undertaken the specific role before but may have experience of similar roles.

An empowering coaching style works well when:

- The coachee is competent and confident.
- The coachee has undertaken the specific task before.
- The coachee has undertaken the specific role before.

CHAPTER 8: INTRODUCING COACHING TO YOUR ENVIRONMENT

In this chapter I discuss:

- How to set up a coaching programme in your IT department.
- Practical advice on how to do this.
- The pitfalls to avoid.

Where to start

So, you have read through the chapters of this book and you are enthused (hopefully) by the concept of coaching. How do you introduce this in your organisation? Where do you begin?

I have seen many IT managers who have wanted to create a culture of coaching in their own department but who have failed at the first hurdle because their culture is one of command and control. Coaching creates an empowering environment but many people can view it as the 'soft' option or lacking in measured improvements.

There are a number of options open to any manager who wants to establish a coaching programme. I have seen this introduced in a number of ways – from managers beginning to coach on a one-to-one basis and getting people interested this way through to the entire management population being trained in coaching techniques.

Gathering data

If you need to gain senior management approval for a programme, it is helpful to gather some data about why the organisation, your department or indeed you need a programme of coaching. This should help you 'sell' the concept of coaching.

You could look, for example, at the data you hold on the existing performance of your team. An alternative is to use the results of any feedback mechanism you have such as 360° feedback to establish a strong need for coaching. Some organisations hold focus groups to establish the appetite for coaching and so that they generate enthusiasm for the programme.

It could be that you can draw on existing customer-satisfaction or employee-satisfaction data to illustrate the need for coaching either in your own department or across the organisation. If you do not already have any measurement in place that you can use, you could, for example, run your own survey.

Employee surveys allow you to assess the level of satisfaction that employees have with their current work environment. You can, for example, embed a question about the appetite for coaching in the survey. Employees across an entire organisation can complete this or it can be used with individual departments or functions. The results will provide a helpful analysis of what is working well and areas for improvement. The outputs should also provide a list of coaching opportunities!

Here is an example of part of an employee satisfaction survey:

The one thing above all others that needs to START happening to make me more satisfied at work is:	
The one thing above all others that needs to CONTINUE happening to make me more satisfied at work is:	
The one thing above all others that needs to STOP happening to make me more satisfied at work is:	

Department name : _____

Thank you for your help. Your responses will be treated in confidence. No one will be identified as part of the results of this survey.

Table 11: Employee satisfaction survey

If you do use this or a similar survey, here are some tips on how you can use the results:

- When you have received the results of the survey, collate them by department.

- Produce a report for each department highlighting their overall satisfaction

- Ensure that the report is circulated to and discussed by all members of the department.

- Encourage each department to set an improvement plan.

- Use the results around coaching to help create a case for a coaching programme.

Self-coaching around establishing a coaching programme

If it is your intention to establish a coaching programme, using the GROW model you can potentially coach yourself around how to do this. Here are some questions that will help you develop a programme. I suggest that you use them selectively. Write down the answers to the questions that seem most relevant to you.

Goal

- What would you like to achieve in terms of a coaching programme for your organisation?
- Specifically what would you like to be different?
- What would you like to happen that is not happening now?
- What would you like not to happen that is happening now?
- What would be a milestone for you?
- What is the minimum or maximum you would accept?
- Is that realistic?
- Will that be of real value to you?

Reality

- What is happening at the moment?
- What effect does this have?
- How often does this happen?
- Apart from yourself, who else is affected?

- What is their perception of the situation?
- What other factors are relevant?
- What have you tried so far?

Options

- What could you do to change the situation?
- What alternatives are there to that approach?
- What approach/actions have you seen used, or used yourself, in similar circumstances?
- Who might be able to help?
- What are the benefits and pitfalls of these options?
- Which actions are of interest to you?

Will/Way Forward

- Which option(s) are you willing to carry out?
- What are the next steps?
- Precisely when will you take them?
- What might get in the way?
- If it did, how would you overcome this?
- Whom do you need to involve?
- When do you intend to involve them?

I hope that by answering these questions you are able to draw up a plan of action that meets your desired outcomes for coaching.

What to watch out for

From experience, if you are developing an in-house programme, there are some pitfalls to avoid. Consider issues of confidentiality. **Do you need to bring in external coaches to kick-start your programme and to ensure that there are sufficient levels of trust?** How can you ensure that if you do run a coaching programme, internal coaches create rapport and trust with their coachees? (My suggestion is that this is strongly communicated in the publicity for the scheme and that it is also a key part of the 'contracting' that takes place with each coachee.)

Do you need to hold taster/induction sessions for the whole of the organisation/department? Often people have a poor understanding of exactly what coaching is and how it differs from counselling or mentoring. From experience we have found that sessions like this tend to break down some preconceptions. Held for an hour or so over a lunchtime or at a convenient time of day, the sessions introduce what coaching is, who can be coached and on what types of topic. They also encourage questions and clarification and are a useful form of publicity for coaching.

What training in coaching skills is required? It is worth considering up front how many people need to be trained as coaches and what your budget for this is. A further consideration is whether you wish your in-house coaches to be accredited. The International Coaching Federation (*www.coachfederation.org*), for example, offers professional qualifications in coaching.

How will you decide who is eligible for coaching? It is worthwhile deciding the criteria by which people can apply for coaching. Is this likely to be open to everyone or can only certain people apply? With some organisations I work with, for example, coaching is only offered to individuals who are on talent programmes. In other organisations coaching is restricted to senior managers. In others again it is open to all.

Will you offer phone coaching as well as face-to-face coaching? If your organisation has a wide spread of geographical locations it is worthwhile offering telephone as well as face-to-face coaching. If so, the coaches you train will need to be adaptable to both media.

How will you provide supervision to coaches? Best practice is to provide supervision to coaches. This is an opportunity on a confidential one-to-one basis for the coach to discuss their coaching sessions and how they are handling the coaching. Importantly the discussion does *not* centre around the content of the coaching that the coach is receiving but rather the interaction between the coach and the coachee. If you do offer this support to internal coaches you will need to set up a coach-supervisor scheme.

How do you manage expectations of the programme? From experience, when a coaching programme begins there can be a lot of pressure on the people involved – both the coach and the coachee – to demonstrate immediate change in behaviour.

As we have seen, **coaching is a process that takes time. It follows the coachee's agenda.** Just as in any change process there are stages that the coachee will go through as they are being coached. Elisabeth Kübler-Ross was a therapist who worked extensively with people who were going through change, often as a result of bereavement. She identified that when people go through change there are a number of distinct reactions:

- Shock – this is the shock that accompanies the realisation that change is going to happen.

- Denial – this is where people tend to ignore the change that is going to happen and continue on as they are.

- Anger – this is the emotion that is felt towards self or others when something has to change.

- Letting go – this is when the individual lets go of their old patterns of behaviour and accepts that change will happen.

- Testing – this is when they test a new behaviour or situation.

- Integration – this is when the new behaviours are integrated into the individual's repertoire of behaviours.

Coachees can go through all these states as they work through the coaching process to reach their goals. Therefore the rate of change cannot be dictated by the organisation. Some people may go through the stages of change within two weeks, others two years. If you set up a company-wide coaching programme, you will need to manage expectations of the results.

What evaluation and measurement of return on investment (ROI) will you use? This question is linked to my last point. In order to 'sell' coaching to the wider organisation you will probably need to demonstrate its ROI. In practice, if you link coaching to some clear measures you may be able to do this. You can use tools such as 360° feedback and client and stakeholder feedback to assist you in this process. You will need to consider at the start of your programme what measures you will use and how you will do this. My suggestion is that you speak to your human resources department who can provide you with assistance and guidance in how to do this.

Summary

This chapter has provided you with an overview of some of the key considerations when introducing a coaching culture. It may have raised more questions than answers, but I hope that it has provided you with some food for thought if you are going to introduce a coaching programme to your organisation.

Finally, I firmly believe that the best advertisement for coaching is to be coached yourself. Once you are a coachee, you will feel the powerful benefits of coaching. In addition, I hope that this book has inspired you to develop your coaching skills so that you can improve the performance and reputation of your IT department.

BIBLIOGRAPHY

Tim Gallwey, *The Inner Game of Tennis*, Pan, 1975, ISBN 978-0-330295-13-0

Julie Hay, *Working It Out at Work*, Sherwood, 1999, ISBN 978-0-95219-64-0

Angus McLeod, *Performance Coaching: The Handbook for Managers, HR Professionals and Coaches*, Crown House Publishing, 2003, ISBN 978-1-904424-05-5

Gladeana McMahon and Averil Leimon, *Performance Coaching for Dummies*, John Wiley & Sons, 2008, ISBN 978-0-470517-48-2

Elisabeth Kübler-Ross, *On Death and Dying*, Routledge, 2008, ISBN 978-0-415463-99-7

J. K. Smart, *Real Coaching and Feedback: How to Help People Improve Their Performance*, Prentice Hall, 2002, ISBN 978-0-273663-28-7

Julie Starr, *The Coaching Manual: The Definitive Guide to the Process, Principles and Skills of Personal Coaching*, Prentice Hall, 2nd edition, 2007, ISBN 978-0-273713-52-4

Sir John Whitmore, *Coaching for Performance: Growing People, Performance and Purpose*, Nicholas Brealey Publishing Ltd, 3rd revised edition, 2002, ISBN 978-1-857883-03-9

Laura Whitworth, Henry Kimsey-House, Karen Kimsey-House and Phil Sandahl, *Co-active Coaching: New Skills for Coaching People Toward Success in Work and Life*, Davies-Black Publishing, 2nd revised edition, 2007, ISBN 978-0-891061-98-4

GLOSSARY

Active listening: Listening in a focused way to what the person is saying and showing that you are listening non-verbally and by summarising, paraphrasing and asking questions.

Body language: The gestures and movements that we use to communicate non-verbally.

Closed questions: A closed question is one that can be answered 'yes' or 'no'.

Coachee: The person who is receiving coaching from the coach.

Developmental feedback: Feedback that focuses on what the individual could do differently and what the manager would like them to improve.

Empowering: A style of coaching that encourages the individual being coached to take responsibility for their own actions and decisions without recourse to the coach.

Feedback: Information given to another person about their performance and behaviour and its impact.

Focus group: A group of individuals who meet to discuss and exchange opinions on a particular topic.

Leading questions: A leading question is when the answer is in the question; for example, 'You are going to send out those tickets today, aren't you?'

Limiting questions: A limiting question is one that gives the recipient some choice; for example, 'What would you like to do first – answer your e-mails or make the calls?'

Glossary

Motivational feedback: Feedback that focuses on what the individual has done well and what the manager would like them to continue.

Open questions: An open question allows you to receive more information than a closed question. Open questions start with what, why, how, when, which or who.

Paraphrase: Using your own words to summarise and go over what the other person has said.

Probe: Ask an open question that uncovers further information from the coachee; for example, 'You say you have little knowledge in this area, what makes you say that?'

Rapport: The relationship of mutual trust and respect between two people.

Reflect back: Using an individual's words to repeat and summarise what they have said.

Reframe: Thinking about a situation in a positive rather than negative way.

ROI: Return on investment.

Self-directed learning: learning that an individual undertakes that they shape and direct themselves.

SMART objectives: Objectives that are Specific, Measurable, Achievable, Realistic and Timebound.

360° feedback: This is a process whereby an individual gathers feedback on their performance. This is collected from their manager, customers, colleagues and other stakeholders, and from direct reports, thus gathering a 360° view of performance.

ITG RESOURCES

IT Governance Ltd sources, creates and delivers products and services to meet the real-world, evolving IT governance needs of today's organisations, directors, managers and practitioners. The ITG website (*www.itgovernance.co.uk*) is the international one-stop-shop for corporate and IT governance information, advice, guidance, books, tools, training and consultancy.

IT Governance products are also available, in local currencies, through

www.itgovernanceusa.com, and

www.itgovernanceasia.com.

Pocket Guides

For full details of the entire range of pocket guides, simply follow the links at *www.itgovernance.co.uk/publishing.aspx*.

Toolkits

ITG's unique range of toolkits includes the IT Governance Framework Toolkit, which contains all the tools and guidance that you will need in order to develop and implement an appropriate IT governance framework for your organisation. Full details are at *www.itgovernance.co.uk/ products/519*.

For a free paper on how to use the proprietary CALDER-MOIR IT Governance Framework, and for a free trial version of the toolkit, see *www.itgovernance.co.uk/calder_moir.aspx*.

Best Practice Reports

ITG's new range of Best Practice Reports is now at: *www.itgovernance.co.uk/best-practice-reports.aspx*. These offer you essential, pertinent, expertly researched information on an increasing number of key issues.

Training and Consultancy

IT Governance also offers training and consultancy services across the entire spectrum of disciplines in the information governance arena. Details of training courses can be accessed at *www.itgovernance.co.uk/training.aspx* and descriptions of our consultancy services can be found at *http://www.itgovernance.co.uk/consulting.aspx*.

Why not contact us to see how we could help you and your organisation?

Newsletter

IT governance is one of the hottest topics in business today, not least because it is also the fastest-moving, so what better way to keep up than by subscribing to ITG's free monthly newsletter *Sentinel*? It provides monthly updates and resources across the whole spectrum of IT governance subject matter, including risk management, information security, ITIL and IT service management, project governance, compliance and so much more. Subscribe for your free copy at: *www.itgovernance.co.uk/newsletter.aspx*.

Lightning Source UK Ltd.
Milton Keynes UK
UKOW02f2157251116

288536UK00001B/257/P